Technology
as a **2nd**
Language

Use Current Technology to
Connect with Your Clients

Domenic DiSario

101 Edition

Here's What's inside

Introduction..5

Dedication...8

Prologue..10

Why Don't Small Business Owners Embrace Technology?.........19

Don't Focus on the Technology, Focus on the Connection.........25

How to Find Out the Preferred Way Your Clients Want to
Communicate...28

Why Embracing Technology May Help You Keep Your Clients and
Possibly Help You Land Your Next One..32

How Technology Is Changing the Face of Business....................36

A Mobile World...41

What You Should Know About Technology but Probably Don't...
....45

How Social Media Can Help Your Business Get More Clients and
Make More Sales...53

How Technology Can Help You Get Closer to Your Clients.........61

Here's a Glimpse of Some of the Technology that Can Connect
You with Your Clients and Future Clients...................................63

Here's a List of Some of the Technology Your Clients Are Using...
....69

Here's How To Get Help and Start Connecting with Your Clients...
....71

Technology as a 2nd Language..77

About the Author..79

Technology as a 2nd language..81

Introduction

March 2014

I often see with my small and medium sized business clients a reluctance to embrace communication technology which is rapidly evolving becoming the new norm. Even worse, I've found more often than not, they don't even know about the business use of the technology. Our clients are embracing these technologies routinely and the pace of adoption can be daunting.

I wanted to find a way to make understanding this technology and fundamental changes in how business is done evident to my clients easily. There is a huge shift in the way this generation of business leaders communicates and it effects how business gets done. This book is a result of that idea.

What follows is an interview where I share with you the dangers you will face if you continue to turn your nose up at this technology. The good news is, catching up isn't as hard as you think.

Enjoy the book!

I hope it changes the way you think about technology and encourages you to take the leap. You may surprise yourself. After all, you've been in business for years and this is an opportunity for greater growth and success.

Warmest Regards,

Domenic DiSario

Name _____

What are some of your ideas?
Use the idea web to jot down your opinion.

❝If you talk to a man in a language he understands, that goes to his head. If you talk to him in his own language, that goes to his heart. ❞

—Nelson Mandela

Dedication

To my wife Debra

And....

"The Team"

"*__There__ is a principle which is a bar against all information, which is proof against all arguments and which cannot fail to keep a man in everlasting ignorance - that principle is contempt prior to investigation.*"

Herbert Spencer

Prologue

It was a beautiful Sunday afternoon in early June of 2013.

Like most Sunday afternoons, my wife Debra and I were walking the dogs. This Sunday we decided to stay close to home and were in the charming New England town of Andover, Massachusetts.

Being in the IT business, it was no big surprise that I got that old familiar "ding" from my iPhone that somebody had just emailed me. Needless to say it was a client looking for a bit of help, and as usual I struggled through the email dialogue with many typos on my side as well as a couple of out of context words. Beware the iPhone autocomplete feature. It can make you look quite foolish.

In any event, I finally got through it and a bit aggravated, I started mumbling to myself. *Why is this so hard. Why am I so clumsy with this.* I have been in technology over 25 years and it always seems I am just a bit behind the curve. I see younger people everywhere effortlessly navigating their smartphones and tablets. And at that moment, I had my "dawn breaks over marblehead" moment and I thought back to the times I tried to learn a new language and how clumsy I felt trying to get the right word in the proper tense and context. And that is what we do when we adopt technology, we learn a second language.

Is this book right for you?

A Quick Quiz .... A word association test.

When I say the word **thumb**, what is the first thing that comes to mind.

1) Something I used to bum a ride 35 years ago
2) To the Lions
3) The Fonz
4) Siskel and Ebert
5) An input device

So if you answered 1 through 4, please read on. This book will teach you how to stay current, valid and competitive in today's business climate utilizing the technologies of today.

If you answered with number 5....Put the book back on the shelf or much more likely, delete it from that shopping cart.

Technology as a 2nd Language...

❝ One language sets you in a corridor for life. Two languages open every door along the way. ❞

–Frank Smith

Susan: We are going to be talking today about your book, *Technology as a 2nd Language: Use Technology to Connect with Your Clients*. I'm curious why you chose to write about Technology as a 2nd Language, Domenic?

Domenic: Susan, I am a habitual late starter. I got started late in business, I got started late in many things in life, including technology, which is my business these days. What I found is it's difficult to adapt to current technologies, especially if you didn't grow up with them. *Technology as a 2nd Language* is the result of me wanting to help others embrace technology in their business as I've seen the positive things that happen when they do and I've seen the opposite of that when they don't embrace technology as well.

To sum it up, to the people who grew up with technology, things look so easy. Tap, tap, tap with the thumb and you're texting 5,000 words a minute. For people who did not grow up with technology, it's a little more difficult. If you're over 45, you're probably hunting and pecking away on that phone rather than the fluid flow of all thumbs like those who grew up with this technology.

I was at a technology conference just last year and I was sitting there listening to a couple of speakers, getting all pumped up. I looked around the room and I noticed I was probably one of the oldest people in the room. I thought, "Well, I'm hearing a lot of great things. I may not even going to get a chance to implement some of this great stuff." But I'm an optimist and thought how can I take advantage of being old? How can I take advantage of my experience? How can I be the youngest old person in the room, rather than the out of date oldest person in the room? That's what brought me to the thought that maybe I should think about coaching and offering technology solutions to a more mature audience.

The second reason I came up with this subject matter was my experience at a ballgame. I was at Fenway Park watching the Red Sox beat the Detroit Tigers. It was especially gratifying because the person I was with was from the Detroit area and a huge fan. Their ace Verlander was on the mound and the Sox were pounding them so it was a good day.

Probably around the fourth or fifth inning, three people came and sat down in front of us. They were probably in their late 20s or early 30s. They sat down and all at once, all three of them whipped out their smartphones, well two smartphones and one of them had a little mini tablet, and almost in unison they started pecking away and pecking away. It was just amazing the speed and dexterity they showed in communicating. Who they were communicating with, I have no idea.

Ten minutes before this I had had an email from one of my clients. It took me about nine minutes to hunt and peck through a six word response. There was a clear difference between my skill set and the skill set of the people in front of me.

As the game went on, we got into a conversation with them. Turned out one of them was a doctor at a local hospital and two of them were hospital administrators, so these were not just college or high school kids. These were professionals. It dawned on me these are the professionals of today not the distant future. I own an IT support company and these are the people that I need to talk to and communicate with right now. I'd better learn how to communicate in a method they like. If not, these folks are not going to want to do business with me. Again, I thought of the challenge of learning a second language as an adult.

Susan: Yes, there's almost a cultural shift happening. The next generation lives and breathes this technology stuff. They don't even think about it, whereas those of us that didn't grow up with technology, well it can be an awkward time. It can be almost like a fish out of water experience to try to use some of this new technology.

Domenic: Exactly right. I went to Paris with my wife five years ago. Naturally, I wanted to learn French as much as I could in the short amount of time that I had. I learned enough to get by but as a second language learner, I was clumsy. A lot of things I said were maybe out of context or in the wrong tense. It was all very awkward. In fact in an effort to tell the waiter that I loved my wife (how this came up, I don't know!) I ended up telling the waiter , I loved him! Although we all had a good laugh, if I had to do business in France, I would be in big trouble. I think older business owners get by but are not as proficient as they can and should be.

❝ The limits of my language are the limits of my world. ❞

–Ludwig Wittgenstein

Why Don't Small Business Owners Embrace Technology?

❝ Learn everything you can, anytime you can, from anyone you can; there will always come a time when you will be grateful you did. ❞

–Sarah Caldwell

Susan: Very good. I can see the analogy there. Why do you think small business owners don't embrace new technology? What's getting in the way?

Domenic: I think most small business owners do embrace technology to the degree where it has worked for them in the past. But what they don't do is embrace the technology that their clients of today are utilizing. I think there are many reasons for this. I think a lot of people don't fully understand it. They're used to successes and having all the answers. Sometimes, for people like us, it's hard to ask the question since you often have to ask someone younger than you are. Sometimes, it takes some courage to be able to ask the question. I think that plays a big part of it. We don't want to look stupid, in other words.

Perhaps other reasons are they don't necessarily see how that pertains to them. If I talk about Twitter or Facebook or LinkedIn or Vine or something that young executives are using today quite naturally, most of the people I talk to wouldn't even know what it was and even if they did know what it was, would think it was not an imperative to use it.

I can analogize back in the old days ... I'm saying the old days, it was only like in, gee, '97, 98 when email was just becoming mainstream for business. I'd have many of these conversations with clients, "But you don't understand. You don't know my people. They will never use email. They need to be on the phone. Faxing's good enough for us." You know, it's funny. I still joke with one of my clients who said just that. I have fun asking him, "So, Paul. You'll never use email, huh?"

Now, if I took their email away for like nine seconds, I'd be getting 100 calls, 50 emails and maybe a few texts from them. I think that holds true for today's executives where they don't really believe that people are going to read a text and give it the same credence as an email. Fifteen years ago, people were saying the same thing about email insisting that business people were not going to give email the same importance as a piece of mail that came from the U.S. Post Office. And for some people, this attitude can work for a while depending on their field and their competition. For example, the former mayor of Boston who retired in 2014 and held office for over 20 years was notorious for not even having a desktop on his desktop. Of course, his successor has real time dashboard technology showing him the state of the city services live. So if you are a beloved elected state official, you probably can get away with not texting. For the rest of us, learn the language or go home!

Susan: Right. Yes and the issue becomes, Domenic, if I'm understanding you correctly, if they don't even know this new technology exists how do they know it's a problem? If they're not on Twitter and they're not on Facebook and they're still running their business just fine, how are they even supposed to know that this is a problem?

Domenic: It's very true and that's the insidiousness of the problem itself. What's the old saying? "I didn't know what I didn't know." Well, if you're reading this book, you're probably at the point that you do know that you don't know something. Intellectually, maybe they don't know it's an issue but I think subconsciously, they do know there is a problem. Who knows what the symptoms might be. Are they losing clients? Maybe they're not losing clients - yet. Maybe they didn't grow the 10, 12 percent that they grew for the last 10 years. Maybe the person they called hasn't returned their call and they're wondering why. Maybe the email they sent hasn't been responded to.

This all could be because this isn't the way their clients are communicating these days. Phone calls and even emails are a very disruptive way of communicating. We know that clients have a different way of communicating because we see our personal communication methods changing. Our families text each other. Celebrities tweet. Senators post to FaceBook.

Let me give you another example of what I use for a barometer for how is this country communicating or maybe how is the world communicating which is the Super Bowl. I consciously take a look at the commercials during the Super Bowl, not so much for the glitz and the humor but to learn about the state of advertising. A lot of them are very sophisticated and very funny but I like to watch because these are all big companies with huge marketing departments and huge budgets. They have their finger on the pulse of how this country is communicating or more to the point, how the country wants to be communicated to.

If I watched the Super Bowl 10 years ago as the Oreo cookie commercial ends, I might see, "For more information call 12345678." Then, five years ago, as that commercial fades out, it might say, "For more info, go to to www.nabisco.com." Last year, I remember watching and everyone had a Facebook tagline as the commercial faded out. This year, Twitter is where it's at. Now 85% of the commercials I saw ended with a simple

Twitter hashtag, #Oreos. That's good information to have. That tells me this is a preferred method of communication these days. Is it just for the people watching the Super Bowl or is it also for your clients and your co-worker?

Susan: I think that's very insightful. You just summed up the truth of the problem. Ten years ago the phone was still the preferred method for reaching clients, then it switched to using your website. Now, we're seeing even websites are not as popular for people always on their phone. They're using apps more than websites. That's very interesting.

Domenic: The target market for these commercials was not young kids either. They were selling new cars, selling beer and selling home insurance. The target market for these Super Bowl commercials was the mature consumer.

Susan: You're saying it wasn't like these commercials were just for 18 year olds just out of high school. You're saying that across the board, this is where people are. For those that aren't on Twitter, we don't even know what that hashtag thing means. We know that maybe it means Twitter, just because it's been pointed out to us, but we have no idea how that translates to how we would even use that to help our business. Shining a light on this is what we're going to be talking about today, right?

Domenic: Yes, absolutely.

Don't Focus on the Technology, Focus on the Connection...

❝ Learning is a treasure that will follow its owner everywhere. ❞

–Chinese Proverb

Susan: What is this "technology" we keep mentioning Domenic? Break it down for us.

Domenic: Technology is such a broad word. Technology might not be the most accurate word either. What we're really talking about here is communication. How am I going to get my message to the person I want to get it to? Communications 101. I have to use the right media. I have to be in context. If I speak English and the person I'm speaking to speaks only Spanish, they're not going to understand what I'm talking about.

We talked about the Super Bowl, so let's talk about the most famous and effective Super Bowl commercial from the 1984 Super Bowl. Apple did the Orwell book *1984* takeoff, destroying Big Brother which was IBM in their eyes back then. That was a great commercial but what if I wasn't watching TV? What if I was listening to the radio? Would I have seen it? No.

Basically, I guess the point here is, I need to use the right messaging mechanism as well as the right medium, if I want to communicate with my client, co-worker or anyone else out there. It isn't about technology, it's about communication. It just so happens, these days, most of the methods of communication are technology based.

How to Find Out the Preferred Way Your Clients Want to Communicate...

Susan: Good point. Yes, if our clients are using an app to communicate and we're sending an email, our message isn't getting through.

Domenic: Yes. And worse than that, if I leave someone a voice mail, it's just an intrusion to them. I'm trying to reach my clients to sell them something. It's going to be less likely that I'm going to get the results I'm looking for if I'm aggravating them by delivering the message in a way they find intrusive.

Susan: Yes, good point.

Domenic: I need to find out the way that they want to communicate. Again, this feels a little clumsy. It's even clumsy for me and I've been in the technology field for more than 25 years. I've learned to adapt and go with the flow, otherwise I wouldn't be in business this long. If I'm sending someone a communication, for me to text it would not be the first thing to pop into my mind as how to reach out. My first thought would probably be an email but it might not be the right thought. I need to understand what the person I'm communicating with, what is their preferred method of communication? I really need to do it their way if I'm going to expect consistent positive results.

Susan: Do you ask them, Domenic? Is that something you can just come out and ask you clients? How do you prefer to communicate? Would you prefer a phone call, Tweet or text?

Domenic: Yes, I ask that question all the time and recommend all business owners start asking their clients that question. Don't assume. You may be surprised at the answer.

Susan: Very good. If you ask your client how do you want to reach them, and they say, "Twitter," and you're not even on Twitter, you've got a problem.

Domenic: Yes. It sounds very complicated but it isn't. If you can dial a phone number, then you can punch in a couple of characters into an email or a text or however that preferred method of communication may be, but you know, what I just described to you, the way I feel, it's a frame of mind. It's in my head. That's the part that we need to transcend. We need to get past this, if we are going to be effective communicators and therefore be successful in the business we are in today.

The purpose of this book is to encourage the easy steps. This is not a 'how to 'book . This is a, "Why is it important?" book, more than a "How you do it," book. We're trying to pass on information as to why it's important, what's available, the what and the why. How you do it is going to be a challenge since communication platforms are a moving target, but we'll save that for the next book.

The old saying, "You need to be aware before you can be effective." We need to create a little awareness. I'm pretty typical I think of the small business owner. I am that person that maybe hasn't embraced technology as much as maybe I should have particularly given the field I'm in. I am that person in their fifties who ran a successful business without these tools and runs a successful business now, but sees some opportunities that just need to be grasped. How do I get past that frame of mind, "Why do I need that? What good is that?

I never needed that in the past. Why do I need it now?" I need it now because my client of today is not my client of yesterday. I need to meet her on her terms, not mine. Relationships are built over 20 years. I'm not saying you're going to lose them because you refuse to Tweet. I am saying after that a relationship of 20 years, when that person retires and you're dealing with their successor, then you become a little vulnerable. Then you want to make sure you're doing everything possible to communicate in a way that the person who buys your product or service is comfortable with.

Why Embracing Technology May Help You Keep Your Clients and Possibly Help You Land Your Next One...

You can never understand one language until you understand at least two.

–Geoffrey Willans

Susan: Yes. Very well said, because the next purchasing agent coming up in line may really resent the voicemail you just left. They may actually roll their eyes at a voicemail because it is as foreign to them as maybe Tweeting is for us. They may just look at that as old fashioned, like the VHS tape is to today's DVD. It just seems so old school. And then maybe it's not too far of a leap to them in thinking your company isn't as progressive as they want to work with and they "go in a different direction".

Domenic: Yes. Also it's a different world. It's a frantic world of hyper-communication. Everything has to be quick, everything has to be fast and everyone has something to say. A person's train of thought and their level of concentration isn't what it used to be. It's not that anyone's less intelligent. There's just so much going on. As a matter of fact, recent studies have indicated that we no longer remember things, we remember where we stored them or where we can retrieve them. Ask a 25 year old the telephone number of their best friend. They won't know it. Their friend is on autodial, they have no need to know it.

Before we started this call, I had to shut off my email and shut off my phone, otherwise you'd be hearing beep bong bop boop and all these other sounds telling me I was getting one of my 900 emails or 64 voice mails for the day.

It's a very busy world. Phone communication, although it has its place, is a thing of the past. That's why the 140 character Tweet, or the 6 second Vine video is an authentic, useful tool.

I was just listening to a webinar on communication, and the presenter said that the human mind processes information four times faster than I can speak that information. What does that really mean? It means unless my content is first, very engaging and interesting or secondly is very short and to the point, I'm going to lose the person on the other side of this conversation.

Susan: Interesting. You're saying by embracing this technology it may help them keep clients and possibly help them land their next client, correct?

Domenic: Without a doubt, yes. They need awareness first. If you don't know it's out there to use, then you can't embrace it.

How Technology Is Changing the Face of Business...

❝ To have another language is to possess a second soul. ❞

–Charlemagne

Susan: Right. This is a wakeup call. In fact, Domenic, you've actually mentioned a couple technologies on this call that I've never heard of. I don't even understand what Vine is so we'll get into that in a minute. It's interesting that if you don't even know that this technology exists, it's impossible to incorporate it into your business. You literally can't do it. The first step is understanding what technology is available. As you say, have an awareness it exists.

Domenic: Yes. And we are doing that right here. As they read my book, they will know more than before they picked it up. You have to understand this technology is available and again, I have to believe most people do know it's available. If you have children, including adult children, you know they no longer use email. They text. They are the same in the workplace. They grudgingly use email but complain that it's inefficient and ineffective. For those of us who remember the 'interoffice memorandum', this is akin to them complaining about the dress code. But that thinking is a mistake. This is a profound change and it is only the beginning of the changes we are likely to see in the near future.

First, you have to know what's out there and what it does and how it can help you. Then, you're going to pick and choose. Maybe Vine is right for your business but not for me. Tumblr is right for me and not for you. You have to do your homework and keep abreast about what communication technology is being used and how and who is using it and why. Otherwise you're not going to be able to make any type of informed decision. We all know it's easier to keep the clientele then to get the next client. But, are we going to get the next wave of clients?

Next time you jump on the train to get home, take a look around. Everyone's banging away on their tablet or phone these days. Mobile is so big, it's just shocking. Worldwide population is around seven billion people. This is worldwide. There are 6,500,000,000 mobile subscriptions worldwide. Now we know not every person in the world has a mobile, but we do know that everyone who can, does and often more than one. There are 350 million people in North America. There are more mobile subscriptions than there are people in North America. That shocked me. Now as a professional in IT, you would not think I could be surprised at this, but because technology is my second language learned as an adult, I'm not as integrated into the mobile world as you might think. This does not mean that all people of a certain age are out of the know. My wife's mother (over 89 years old) binge watches TV on her tablet. So if I'm an advertiser, how will I advertise to an audience who watches content only on You Tube and who would not even consider subscribing to cable.

Susan: I know five year olds that have a tablet.

Domenic: Without a doubt. You see even younger as well. We're talking about the young but the preferred device for a 75 year old person is a tablet, believe it or not. More in fact, than a laptop. When you think about it, I was surprised to see this, but when you think about it, it's a very simple device. You can only do a few things but you can do the important things. You can email, you can watch a movie, you can read a book, you can...

Susan: Get on Facebook. Yes.

Domenic: Get on Facebook. Facebook is an interesting opportunity. I think there are over 1,000,000,000 Facebook users and close to 75% of Internet users in the $75,000 plus salary range are Facebook users. The numbers boggle my mind. But even here, the demographics are changing. Facebook is not seeing an increase in users under 30. They have all moved on to the next thing. But plenty of consumers use Facebook and for some, its where they start their day.

A Mobile World

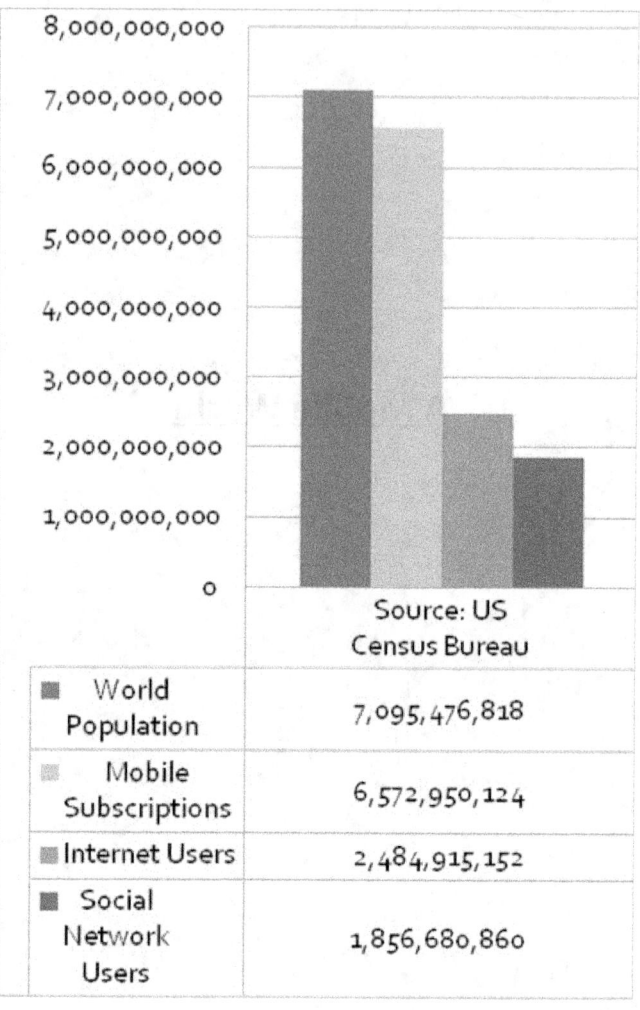

World Population	7,095,476,818
Mobile Subscriptions	6,572,950,124
Internet Users	2,484,915,152
Social Network Users	1,856,680,860

Source: US Census Bureau

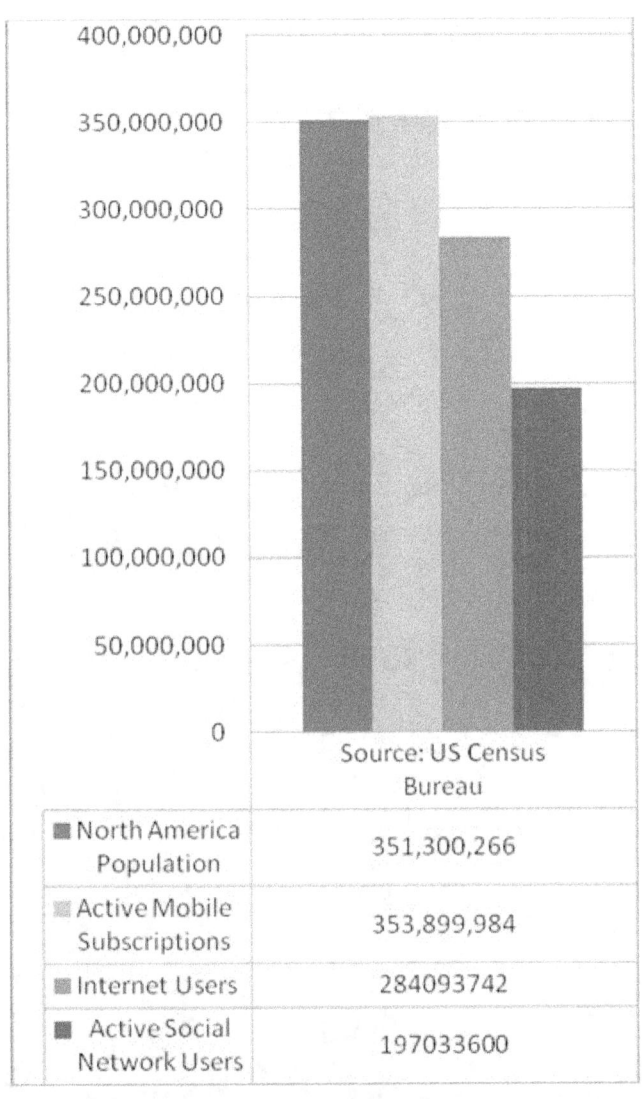

■ North America Population	351,300,266
■ Active Mobile Subscriptions	353,899,984
■ Internet Users	284093742
■ Active Social Network Users	197033600

Source: US Census Bureau

North America-More Subscriptions Than People

❝ Those who know nothing of foreign languages know nothing of their own. ❞

–Johann Wolfgang von Goethe

What You Should Know About Technology but Probably Don't...

“ Language is the road map of a culture. It tells you where its people come from and where they are going. ”

–Rita Mae Brown

Susan: What are some things about technology that business owners should know about that they're not even aware of?

Domenic: Sure. First, they should be aware of how huge tablet computing is. Mobile consists of all devices from your smartphone which after all is another computer in your pocket. So, you have your smartphone, your tablets and your convertible hybrid devices which are a laptop one second and a tablet after you detach the keyboard.

In 2014, there will be more tablets sold than desktops and laptops combined. That's what computing looks like tomorrow.

In my business we do something called Q.B.R.s which are quarterly business reviews. We're in the IT service business, so we go in and talk about next year's budget. We might talk about the latest applications that might benefit the client. We talk about the newest methods of communication across platforms to benefit the client. I was just with a C.P.A. firm and we were talking about iPads. I think the iPad Minis might have just been introduced but for whatever reason, we were talking about iPads. Astonishingly, I got the same pushback as I got with the email group from the 90s. "iPad? What good is an iPad? Who in my company would ever use an iPad?"

What can you say to this very smart business owner but "Who would use an iPad? Your next hire will. That might be the only device they would consider worthwhile. As a matter of fact, it may be their own personal device that they want to use as a work tool. As time goes by, it's more and more of a possibility and we have to be prepared to create the protocols that allow for workers to use the most efficient technology for themselves because they will demand the choice.

Susan: Right

Domenic: Companies have to prepare for the influx of handheld technology. This year, it's 50/50 between tablets and PCs and desktops. By 2017, you're probably going to sell three tablets for every PC.

Its not only that we're not going to always hire people of the same generation as we are and we're not always going to do business with people of the same generation. The takeaway is that cross platform communication and nonstandard devices are the norm not the exception. It's not complicated to manage this. In truth, it's no harder than anything else we've ever learned. We just need to know what is available, what people use, and we can leverage this new world to get to the next level of business success.

Susan: These small business owners, they have a certain budget for technology and they may just assume that they need to replace their desktops with more desktops and you're saying, "Hmm. Maybe that's not the case any longer." We may want to relook at this. Not everybody is going to want to work from a PC. Some, as you say, your next new hire for example, may want to work from a tablet. The business owner needs to be aware of this and start considering this. I think that's actually a very important observation.

Domenic: Yes. It's happening all day long. We have a bunch of clients in the medical field and all the doctors have iPads. That's how they're doing patient documentation. If you're going to do online banking, most people are still more comfortable at the desktop or a laptop. Yet, if you're going to read a book or do social media or even email these days, the preferred method is tablet or even phone. The phone is just a smaller tablet if you think about it, especially the iPhones or the newer Droid phones.

"A different language is a different vision of life."

-*Federico Fellini*

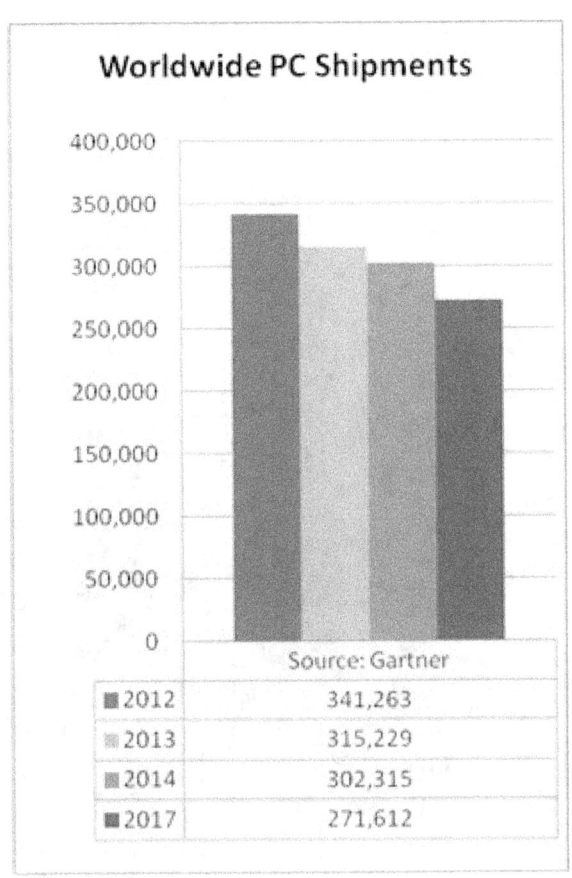

Worldwide PC Shipments	
Source: Gartner	
2012	341,263
2013	315,229
2014	302,315
2017	271,612

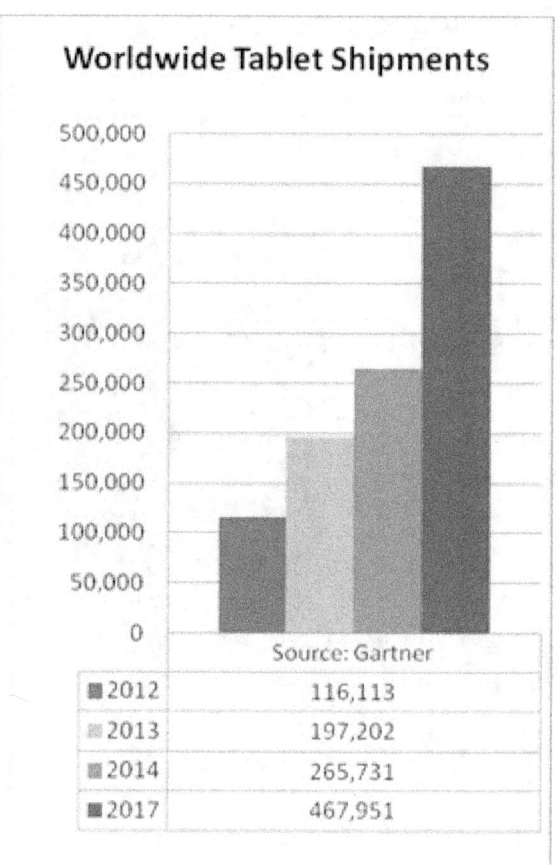

Worldwide Tablet Shipments

Source: Gartner

Year	Shipments
2012	116,113
2013	197,202
2014	265,731
2017	467,951

How Social Media Can Help Your Business Get More Clients and Make More Sales...

❝ Language is the blood of the soul into which thoughts run and out of which they grow. ❞

–Oliver Wendell Holmes

Susan: Very good. Can we, Domenic, talk about some of the things you mentioned earlier that I didn't understand? I know social media is a term that's tossed around a lot. I think people understand Facebook now. It's been around long enough and they may understand basically what Twitter is but social media is this catchall that means what? It's a way to communicate socially with your friends. Is that how you would describe it?.

Domenic: Yes. I think it's been misnamed. That's how social media cut its teeth. Facebook used to be called, "The Facebook," started at Harvard as a way to keep tabs on your friends and classmates. Then it got adopted into business.

Today, believe it or not as I said, as popular as Facebook is most of its new subscribers are with a more older user. Right now, Facebook is yesterday's technology to the young people, not to people that I want to be talking with. I'm talking about the 25 and under. Facebook is yesterday, right?

Susan: Old news.

Domenic: Yes. Instagram and Tumblr are the new Facebook for the younger generation. What's very big and plays well from a business point of view is video. YouTube is huge. I understand that behind Google, YouTube is the most searched platform in the world. People can spend days, weeks looking at silly YouTube videos but if you look at training and you look at a lot of marketing and such, it's all YouTube based. Most video is housed in YouTube. Vine, as I mentioned earlier is the Twitter of video. Vine is simply a short six second video.

Susan: You say it's six or seven seconds, that's all?

Domenic: Six seconds and you can say a lot. What can you say in 140 characters in Twitter? Enough to buy every marketing dollar in the Super Bowl.

Vine was bought by Twitter since they keep a close eye on the market and saw this as an a compatible technology. You create a quick six second video. It could be anything and is ideal to send around to your phone friends.

Susan: Yes. It seems to me that there's almost a business shift because how you get your next wave of clients may be coming right through this social media and not through traditional methods. I think people are just like you pointed out earlier, they scoff at voicemail now. Well, maybe they're scoffing at your direct mail campaign or your postcard or things like that. Using social media to reach new clients, actually, I think is what you mean when you say it's big business. This is how people learn and refer services and products. Their friend recommended and their friend mentioned that they just did something. Isn't that why it's so important?

Domenic: It is big business. What's the old saying? "People do business with people they like," right?

Susan: Right.

Domenic: How does someone get to like me? They have to get to know me. How do they get to know me? The old days, how did you do business? Do you go out and play 18 on the golf course or go to a basketball game with one of your clients? I had one client who used to buy season tickets for the Red Sox. I give out a few Bruins tickets to a few of the clients. Maybe I accompany them. Go out to dinner. These are all social behaviors. The key component is that we base our relationships on common ground and what is a more basic commonality than language.

"Language is not a genetic gift, it is a social gift. Learning a new language is becoming a member of the club -the community of speakers of that language."

–*Frank Smith*

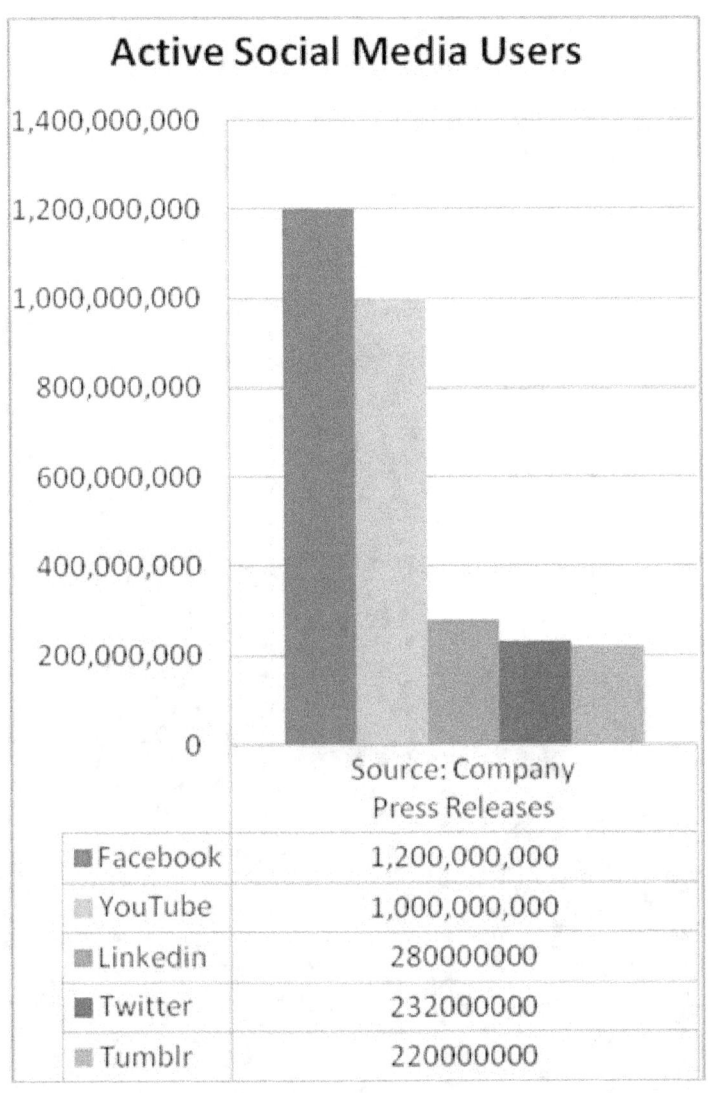

Active Social Media Users

▦ Facebook	1,200,000,000
▦ YouTube	1,000,000,000
▦ Linkedin	280000000
▦ Twitter	232000000
▦ Tumblr	220000000

Source: Company Press Releases

Facebook Still Rules – For Now

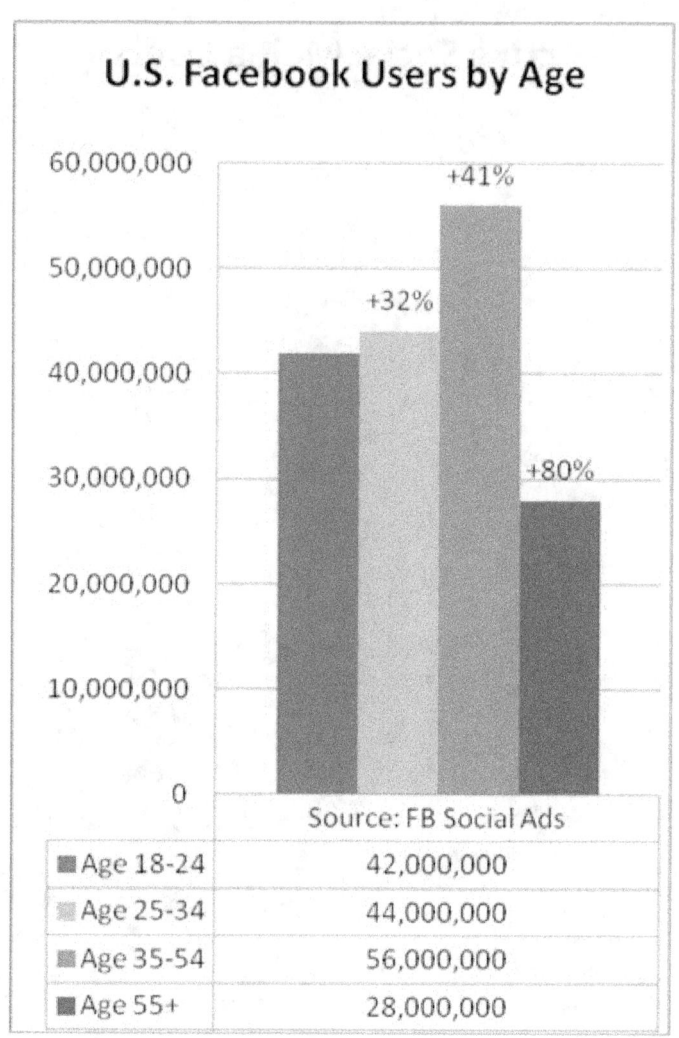

U.S. Facebook Users by Age

■ Age 18-24	42,000,000
■ Age 25-34	44,000,000
■ Age 35-54	56,000,000
■ Age 55+	28,000,000

Source: FB Social Ads

+41%
+32%
+80%

Facebook Becoming a "Mature" Platform

How Technology Can Help You Get Closer to Your Clients...

Susan: Right.

Domenic: Social media is just a way to get a little bit closer to your client. I'm a sales and marketing enthusiast. I'm very intrigued about why people make the decisions they make and how those decisions can be effected. Gary Vaynerchuk wrote a book called *The Thank You Economy* a few years ago. He emphasized that people are going to do business with people they like and they're going to like me when they get to know me. My ethical goal is formulate a relationship where I'm giving more than I'm getting and that each one of us in the relationship shares commonality. Nothing says familiarity like YouTube!

Social media is an easy way to give. I might give a free training on YouTube. I might Tweet out a link to this interesting article on the new tax laws in Massachusetts. I might Tweet that out to my group of clients that are CPA's. There are many ways to use this but I guess first you have to understand what it is. You also have to understand that it's no different than what we did yesterday fundamentally. It's only different functionally. How we do it is different, but the reason we do it, to get closer to our clients, is still the same.

People always want to do business with people they know and like. This just a different way for people to get to know and like you. If you look back at the different types of relationships you had with clients you always want to do business with people that you have some commonality with. Social media is one of the ways to get commonality.

Here's a Glimpse of Some of the Technology that Can Connect You with Your Clients and Future Clients...

"Americans who travel abroad for the first time are often shocked to discover that, despite all the progress that has been made in the last 30 years, many foreign people still speak in foreign languages."

–*Dave Barry*

Susan: Very good. It's very helpful. Recently I called a younger client to discuss something on a deal. He actually asked me, "Why did you call me? It wasn't an emergency." I was taken aback. Here I thought it was good that I reached out and called him, so we could connect and such, but he called me out on it, like, "Don't call me unless it's an emergency and even then, I prefer you to send a text."

It's a new world. They have a different mindset but that's the future. That's where we're headed. I think what you're doing here is very, very important because you're shining a light on things that as we said to start the call, things that businesses are not even aware of. It's like you said. They have a sense that something's off. Maybe sales are down and one of the reasons may be because you are still trying to communicate with your clients in a way that no longer works for them. Maybe we should stop and look at that.

Domenic: Without a doubt. Another big switch which I have to talk about is the cloud. Cloud storage is a basic business tool and it's something that we can consider as the foundation for all these communication methods because all these applications are in the cloud. YouTube is in the cloud. The Twitter databases are in the cloud. Facebook is in the cloud. All the banking you do is in the cloud. I know you personally use Google Docs, right? That's in the cloud.

Curiously, even the earliest mass applications like AOL were stored in the cloud. People just did not refer to this as being in the cloud which just means that the app is not stored locally in your house on your personal desktop. These storage locations are banks of large systems called file servers which have significant redundancy which guarantees they will be functioning all the time. Now, storage in the cloud is a bona fide service offering. As business opt to store information on internet based resources and not on local computer or local File servers, 'working from home' is more efficient. It's cheaper for the company. But home based workers need to communicate. Enter SKYPE and GoToMeeting. SKYPE, a voice communication service is free, reliable and has moved us closer to the wonderful world of "The Jetsons." GoToMeeting is transforming how business meetings are being done remotely. These communication services are child's play to the Millennials as they should be for us

So you see, as more people buy into the cloud, application development and deployment is faster and cheaper. The apps easier to develop, they're easier to roll out, they're easier to sell in market. Anyone with an idea and a little technical programming knowledge can get an app to market. This is the age of innovation on steroids. And workers want to have personally configured systems. The distinction between work computer and personal computing is completely blurred. In fact there is no longer any meaningful distinction.

The other interesting innovation in my opinion that is really important comes from   Bill Gates in his book *Business @ the Speed of Thought*. He told this story. The milk in the refrigerator is nine days old. Soon that milk carton is going to have a way to communicate that to you. Maybe it's going to send you a text. He talked about getting a phone call saying, "Time to replace me. I'm getting sour," type of thing. That sounded all futuristic and a little silly back then (1999) but when you think about it today, that's exactly what's happening. Everything is going to be identifiable with an IP address or an RFID code. It's already happening in your car, your phone and even your thermostat in your home. This is how these tracking systems work. That's why I can press a button in my car and I can get instant help from my GPS which knows where I am. This is how I set my thermostat remotely.

Not only is every device is going to be identifiable. Even experiences can be identifiable. So not only can each product can be tracked, you can barcode the product so that the consumer can instantly provide feedback on an instant survey by simply scanning the barcode with their phone.

Again, communication is driving these innovations. For business, it's great to have your equipment barcoded and perhaps maintained remotely, but the real win is knowing what the user thinks. If you are not obtaining customer feedback, you will absolutely go out of business (unless you are the government and then of course, you just get bigger and spend more money!). There is no excuse for not understanding this new language. Technology is the Latin of the modern world. We all have to speak it to thrive.

This very connected world is not futuristic any more. I don't want to get technical but there's something called an IP Address. That stands for Internet Protocol Address. It is a numeric representation of a resource and is pretty much how your email's identified or your website is identified. Your web address might be www.susan.com but underneath that is a number. 173.xxx.xxx.xxx . There are so many devices in use that we've run out of I P addresses.

Susan: Wow. Did not know that.

Domenic: IPv6 is the next iteration of the IP addressing structure. There's not enough IP addresses to give every milk carton and loaf of bread its own IP these days. There's a huge engineering effort going on to rectify this issue and it's already in play. Some enterprises are already using this new addressing structure.

You can analogize that situation to our phones or more specifically the way we use phone numbers. It used to be seven numbers and then they had to tack on an area code because those seven numbers weren't enough to identify every phone. Think of IPv6 like that, there weren't enough numbers so they had to make more addresses available and the way that was done was by making the addresses longer.

Susan: Like our license plates.

Domenic: Pretty much, but I guess my point is that it's becoming a very small world linked with technology, driven by communication needs.

Here's a List of Some of the Technology Your Clients Are Using...

Susan: Can you share a list of the technology at a glance for us Domenic? I know, as you said this is more of a "Why Book", than a "How To Book", but can you share with us a list of some of the technology so we can see at a glance what we don't know?

Domenic: Sure. Here you are. Here is a list of technology that clients are using to communicate. It's a big list, but it's not as scary as it seems once you understand how they work. In no particular order:

• Facebook	• Google Hangouts
• Twitter	• Google Docs
• Linked In	• Snapchat
• Skype	• Dropbox
• Pinterest	• YouTube
• Vine	• Whatsapp

I am going to guess that most businesses use LinkedIn and DropBox. Some may have ventured to YouTube. The smart ones are leveraging every platform above which in most cases are FREE!

**Here's How To Get Help and Start Connecting
with Your Clients...**

Language is not a genetic gift, it is a social gift. Learning a new language is becoming a member of the club -the community of speakers of that language."

—Frank Smith

Susan: Wow. Life really is changing isn't it? If someone wants help in this area, if somebody reads this and decides that they need more help in this area, how can they reach you, Domenic?

Domenic: All the information they need to get started is on my website which is freely offered. The best way is to connect to my website at www.technologyasa2ndlanguage.com.

Susan: Okay. And If they wanted to hire you, I assume you're available for that?

Domenic: Absolutely. We do a lot of presentations for local chambers and rotaries as well as hosting lunch and learns. We'd be happy to come in and talk to a group at your company. Any and all of that. We also do one on ones if requested.

Susan: Start embracing some of this technology, like you said, it may be a little bit overwhelming at first glance, but weirdly enough, it could be that they incorporate a couple of these new things and they find they save time.

Domenic: I can tell you this. It looks undoable. But, give me one hour of your time and there'll be enough clarity to get you started. After that, you will know in which direction you need to go. The strategy can be different for every company and it depends on what the goals are.

Susan: Okay. That's good. This doesn't have to be daunting. It doesn't have to be this ordeal. Just give you a ring and you'll be able to point them in the right direction.

Domenic: It's going to seem too new, but think about the first time we rode a bike. We couldn't do it. We couldn't do it. We couldn't do it. We would never do it and then we did it and what was so hard about that, right?

Susan: Very well said. Very good. Any last thoughts for folks?

Domenic: Feel free to give us a call or an email. Now, I'm actually going against my own advice. Perhaps I should say, give us a Tweet or a Text. Check us out.

There is a lot of information out on our website. Again, it's all free. Start there. Open the first door. It can seem daunting but it isn't. You've got to take the first step. When you do, you find that it's not as tough as you thought.

Susan: This can be a nice turning point for the businesses. Maybe they've been looking at this as a negative, an expense if you will to the organization but it actually can be a real positive to the bottom line for them.

Domenic: It's definitely a positive. This is just common sense, especially when I think back to Fenway Park and seeing those three young people in front of me using technology in a way I don't see some small business adopting. And in retrospect, they weren't so young after all. One of them was a doctor. Couldn't be too young. This is a group of people I'm going to be communicating with today and tomorrow. I better learn to do it in a way that they prefer if I want to do business with them. This is now, not tomorrow.

What is the best way to learn a new language. It's by immersing yourself with people that speak it every day. You learn the basic verbal structure, add a couple of adjectives and you can successfully ask for a cup of coffee. Do a little bit more and you can get your coffee exactly the way you like it!

Susan: It's been great having you shine a light on this Domenic. I think it's a topic that may not be near and dear to people's hearts but it should be.

Domenic: It will be.

Susan: There you go. (Laughs)

Domenic: All right, Susan. It's been a pleasure. Thank you very much.

"A man who knows two languages is worth two men."

—French Proverb

Technology as a 2nd Language

The story behind the story

This book was originally slated to be a 200 page or so offering, covering a multitude of topics pertaining to utilizing various technologies for the more "mature" audience. After lots of give and take with various parties, it was decided that we should break this apart into several much shorter books. The first one, which you just read, emphasizing the "What" and the "Why" with subsequent books focusing on the "How".

So in the spirit of that strategy, I would like to ask you to keep your eyes open for the next two volumes of the "Technology as a 2nd Language" series.

Technology as a 2nd Language: The Social Media Edition

And

Technology as a 2nd Language: The Cloud Edition

Both will be released this summer (Summer of 2014)

Thanks and have a great day,

Dom

"You live a new life for every new language you speak. If you know only one language, you live only once."

—*Czech proverb*

About the Author

Offering over 25 years of experience in the information technology field, Mr. DiSario is the President of Business Solutions Unplugged, Inc. He has worked his way up through the industry starting out in the early 1980's as a PC technician. He became a Certified NetWare Engineer (CNE) and has designed and implemented PC Networks and vertical solutions since 1988. While he was an independent contractor for a number of network service companies, he went on to become one of the first Novell Master CNE's in the area. In the late eighties he began accruing his own client base, many of whom remain clients today.

As Microsoft entered the networking market, Domenic enhanced his skills to mirror the changing technology and became a Microsoft Certified Systems Engineer (MCSE), as well as an HP Accredited Systems Engineer, a Citrix Certified Engineer and a Microsoft Certified Trainer (MCT).

Mr. DiSario is recognized as an industry leader in local and wide area networking as well as Cloud Solutions, remote access solutions and satellite office connectivity for both large and small companies. He has lectured on networking at Boston University, served as adjunct faculty at Clark University, and has been published in LAN Times. His company has also been featured on WCVB TV's Chronicle.

"Change your language and you change your thoughts."

—*Karl Albrecht*

Technology as a 2nd language

The 101 Edition

Use Current Technology to Connect with Your Clients

Maybe you've noticed that your clients just aren't as reachable as they used to be. They are not picking up the phone or responding to your voicemails. Maybe you've even lost a few key clients and don't know exactly why. They suddenly go dark on you and the next thing you know they are doing business elsewhere. You've been in business for years. What's going on?

You've heard about this social media thing but haven't embraced it as you've been successful for years without it, so why bother?

In fact, you don't even understand what this technology is. You don't know what a Tweet is and you doubt you'd ever want to know. You think being able to reach your clients by phone and email should continue to be enough because it's worked for your business in the past.

But you know what? It's not. The next, and for that matter, the current generation of business leaders are digital wizards. The next purchasing agent you try to speak to probably won't even answer their phone and don't expect them to listen to or return a voice-mail. It's just not how they communicate and if you don't figure out how they do communicate and meet them there, you won't be who they reach out to when they need help.

It's happening more and more. Clients are making huge buying decisions over text messages. Every month new ways to communicate are being developed and your business needs to have at least a rudimentary understanding of them or your sales will drop and profits will suffer.

If this is ringing a bell, if any of this resonates, if you'd like help in figuring out this new technology, I say you are in the right place. And the good news is it's easier than you think.

Here's 3 ways we can help you right now:

1) We could speak at your next group or company meeting.

2) We provide One on One consultation/coaching services for your business.

3) Or visit our website: technologyas2ndlanguage.com for more information.

If you'd like us to help, just send an email to: info@technologyasa2ndlanguage.com.

Look to this Day

Look to this day, for it is life,
The very life of life,
In its brief course lies all the realities
And verities of existence:
The bliss of growth, the splendor of action,
The glory of power.

For yesterday is but a dream
And tomorrow is only a vision.
But today, well lived, makes every yesterday
A dream of happiness!
And every tomorrow a vision of hope.
Look well, therefore, to this day!

~Sanskrit Proverb~